D1390152

ART · FROM · THE · PAST

The GREEKS

GILLIAN CHAPMAN

GENERAL CRAFT TIPS AND SAFETY PRECAUTIONS

Read the instructions carefully first, then collect together everything you need before you start work.

It helps to plan your design out first on rough paper.

If you are working with papier mâché or paint, cover the work surfaces with newspaper.

Always use a cutting mat when cutting with a craft knife and ask an adult to help if you are using sharp tools.

Keep paint and glue brushes separate and always wash them out after use. Use non-toxic paints and glue.

Don't be impatient – make sure plaster is set, and papier mâché and paint are thoroughly dry before moving on to the next stage!

All projects make perfect presents!
Try to make them as carefully as you can.

RECYCLING

Start collecting materials for craftwork. Save newspaper, clean coloured paper and card, cardboard boxes and tubes of different sizes, glossy paper and gift wrap, and scraps of string and ribbon.

Clean plastic containers and old utensils are perfect for mixing plaster and making paper pulp.

PICTURE CREDITS

AKG Photos: /Erich Lessing 6 bottom left, 36, /John Hios 6 bottom right: **British Museum:** 20, 22, 32, 34; **C M Dixon:** 7 top left; **Michael Holford:** 7 bottom left, 8 top right, 8 bottom right, 8 bottom left, 10, 12, 14, 16, 18, 26; **Piraeus Museum, Athens:** 24; **Robert Harding:** 7 bottom right; **Science Photo Library:** /John Sanford & David Parker 28; **Sonia Halliday Photographs:** /F H C Birch 30.

Photographer: Rupert Horrox
Illustrator: Teri Gower, Picture Researcher: Jennie Karrach

This edition published in 2006 by Fernleigh Books,
1A London Road, Enfield, Middlesex, EN2 6BN

Copyright ©1998 Fernleigh Books

All rights reserved.

ISBN 1 905212 36 4

Printed in China

The author and Fernleigh Books would like to thank
Keith Chapman for all his help with the model making.

ART · FROM · THE · PAST

The GREEKS

GILLIAN CHAPMAN

THE GREEK EMPIRE

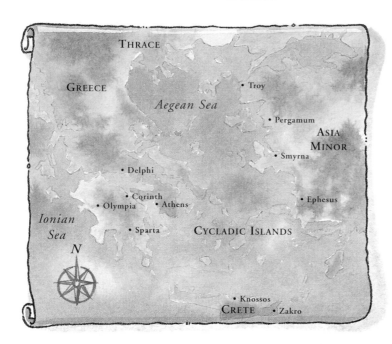

THE LAND OF ANCIENT GREECE was made up of a hot, mountainous **peninsula**, surrounded by hundreds of small islands. Small isolated communities grew up all over this area, often cut off from each other by sea or mountains. These small communities grew into the Greek states, which consisted of a city supported by the surrounding countryside. Each independent state had its own laws and government.

Although the states, such as Athens and Sparta, were constantly quarrelling amongst themselves, they were all united as Greeks. They all spoke the same language, worshipped the same gods and shared the same customs. They became a strong united force when they fought a common enemy, such as the victorious war against the Persians.

LEFT. *The city of Ephesus, in Asia Minor, had a huge sanctuary dedicated to Artemis, the Greek goddess of hunting.*

BELOW. **Athens** *was the most powerful city state and the Athenians built temples to their gods on the* **Acropolis***.*

6

LAW, ORDER AND KNOWLEDGE

ABOVE. **Aristotle** (384–322 BC) had a great love of knowledge. He was a politician, poet, scientist and philosopher.

The idea of a **democratic** government was a Greek concept. The first democracy was established in Athens in 508 BC. The Greeks enjoyed an ordered society in which individuals had great freedom and power. Creative thinking and personal achievements were encouraged. They admired the complete man – someone who was equally talented as an athlete, a poet or a philosopher.

The Greeks excelled in many scientific areas, such as astronomy, mathematics and **philosophy**, which is the love of knowledge. They were a sea-faring nation and needed the knowledge of astronomy for navigation. Greek architects relied on laws of geometry and mathematics for their engineering and building. Their styles of architecture have influenced many cultures that have followed after them.

LEFT. The treasury of the Athenians at Delphi.

BELOW. Fallen column drums at Athens show how the huge columns were constructed in sections.

ARTS AND CRAFTS

THE GREEK LOVE OF BEAUTY shows itself in their art and architecture. Sculpture was created in honour of the gods and was displayed in temples and public buildings. It showed a perfect view of life – men with strong healthy bodies, beautiful women draped in fine clothes, and strong horses carrying brave warriors. Skilled sculptors and artisans worked for patrons that demanded very high standards.

Poets were also held in high esteem and the language of poetry, often set to music, developed into the high forms of literature and theatre which are still greatly admired today. Ancient legends and poems were memorised and passed on by storytellers. The most famous legends were written down by Homer in the *Iliad* and the *Odyssey*, and historians now believe that many of these epic tales are based on fact.

RIGHT. *A caryatid figure from the Erechtheum, the temple of Athena on the* **Acropolis** *at* **Athens***.*

BELOW LEFT. *The 4th century BC theatre at Delphi.*

BELOW RIGHT. *Vase painting of the legends of Homer.*

8

GREEK CRAFT TIPS

Painting and finishing projects is exciting. It is the most difficult part, so take your time. By following these simple painting tips everyone will be happy with the results.

Paint the masks in a dark colour and leave to dry. Brush a lighter colour on, leaving some of the dark paint showing through. Finally brush with gold paint to get a special effect.

Build up layers of different coloured paint to achieve brilliant effects. Keep the brush dry and use the paint sparingly. Don't draw in all the details if you don't want to!

Greek craftsmen were clever, but not at everything! Vases were made by a potter, but painted by an artist. When you paint pictures on a project, draw out the design first.

Don't be afraid to rub out or start again. Only trace onto the project when the design looks right. Fix the tracing paper with tape to stop it moving while you are tracing down.

The Greeks believed that if something was worth doing, it was worth doing well. In this same spirit, try to make your projects as carefully as you can.

DOLPHIN FRESCOE

THE WALLS OF MANY TEMPLES and palaces were once decorated with beautiful **frescoes**. Originally these scenes were painted directly into the wet plaster. However, over the centuries they have become damaged and many have been restored by modern artists, copying fragments of thc original paintings.

There are many remains at the **Minoan** royal palace on Knossos, an island of **Crete**. This fresco decorates the walls of the Queen's apartment.

The ancient Greek world was made up of the mainland of Greece, with its rugged coastline and many islands. Dolphins were often sighted in the warm coastal waters.

DOLPHIN FRESCO

YOU WILL NEED

Cardboard	Newspaper
Paper & pencil	String & scissors
Tracing paper	Poster paints
Ruler & sticky tape	Fine paint brush
Cutting mat	Plaster, an old container
Craft knife	& mixing utensils

1. Work out your design on rough paper following the ideas shown here. Copy the dolphins and the border patterns on the fresco.

2. Measure the design and make a cardboard mould the same size, with sides 5 cm deep. Score the sides, turn them up and tape together.

3. Mix up the plaster in an old container, following the instructions on the packet. Pour the plaster into the mould to a depth of 3 cm.

4. Smooth the surface of the plaster. Cut a 15 cm length of string and push the ends into the wet plaster, leaving a loop to hang the fresco up when it is dry.

5. When the plaster is dry carefully remove it from the mould. Trace down your dolphin design onto the smooth surface and pencil in the outlines.

6. Following the pencil outlines, carefully colour in the dolphin design using poster paints and a fine brush. Try copying the colour scheme of the original fresco (far left).

11

GOLDEN TREASURE

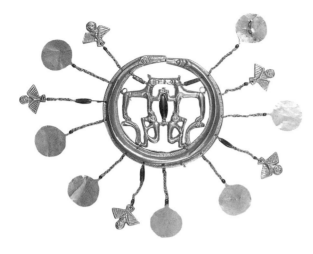

Look carefully at the earring above and see the dogs, owls, monkeys and snake that shape the design.

THE GREEKS ADMIRED BEAUTIFUL SCULPTURE, works of art – and beautiful people. But physical beauty was for the wealthy. Men kept their bodies healthy and strong through sport. Rich women wore fine clothes, perfume and gold jewellery.

This golden earring is part of a collection of jewellery called the Aigina Treasure. The treasure was named after the Greek island where it was found. The treasure includes bracelets, brooches and belts. It was made by skilled goldsmiths in about 1700 BC from beaten gold, gold wire and precious stones.

GOLDEN CHARM BRACELET

YOU WILL NEED
Gold poster paint	Empty sticky tape roll
Gold beads	Gold thread & needle
White tissue paper	Scraps of stiff card
PVA glue & brush	Scissors & pencil

1. Brush PVA glue over an area of the empty sticky tape roll, then stick small pieces of white tissue paper to it.

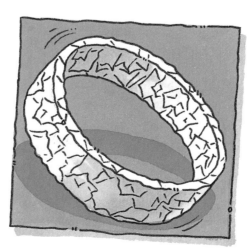

2. Completely cover both sides of the roll with several layers of the glued tissue pieces and leave to dry.

3. Cut out a number of shapes from the card – circles, stars, diamonds, moons. Make a hole in each with the needle.

4. Paint the textured roll with gold poster paint and then paint all the card shapes on both sides.

5. Sew a length of gold thread through each charm. Attach gold beads to the thread and tie each thread to the bracelet.

6. Make some more charms and tie them to a pair of gold earrings so they match the charm bracelet.

Try making a charm bracelet for someone special.

Shape the charms to suit different people by using animal or flower shapes.

GLOSSARY

Acropolis – a defensive fort or citadel usually built on the highest point of a city. The hill top acropolis in **Athens** is also where the Athenians built their temples to the gods.

Aristotle – a Greek politician and philosopher who lived between 384 and 322 BC.

Athens – the most important and wealthiest city state in ancient Greece, famed as a centre for art and culture.

Crete – the largest island in the Aegean Sea that formed part of Ancient Greece.

Democracy – a state or country that is ruled by the people where they vote for a leader. This type of government was first utilised in the Greek city states.

Fresco – a large painting decorating walls or ceilings, made by applying paint directly into the wet plaster.

Hippocrates – a Greek doctor who lived between 460 and 377 BC. He believed in treating the whole body and is known as the founder of modern medicine.

Hoplites – well-armed foot soldiers of the Greek army.

Labyrinth – a large maze. The labyrinth on **Crete** was the home of the Minotaur and was impossible to escape from.

Mediterranean – the name given to the sea and the lands and countries surrounding it.

Medusa – a **mythological** creature. One of the Gorgons, it was half woman – half serpent, whose hair was full of writhing snakes and whose gaze turned men to stone.

Minoan – the ancient civilisation on **Crete**. It was named after its king, Minos, and reached its peak between 2200 and 1450 BC.

Mythological – fictional stories about gods and heroes that have been retold through time.

Odysseus – a Greek hero, whose adventures, including the capture of **Troy**, were written down by Homer.

Olympia – the Greek city that held the athletic games in honour of **Zeus** every 4 years.

Parthenon – large temple built on the **Acropolis** for the goddess Athena.

Peninsula – an area of land that is almost surrounded by sea, but remains connected to the mainland.

Philosophy – the study of the love of knowledge and wisdom.

Proportion – Greek sculptors devised ways of measuring the body so every part looked perfect and was in proportion to the whole.

Ptolemy – a Greek astronomer. In c.100 AD he used mathematics to explain the movement of the planets.

Realism – a style of art where sculpture and painting is made to look as realistic as possible.

Sickle – a sharp curved tool used to cut straw and wheat.

Terracotta – word meaning 'burnt earth'. Terracotta is a form of red clay used for making pottery.

Theseus – the young prince of **Athens**, who killed the Minotaur in the **Labyrinth**.

Troy – an ancient city on the west coast of modern Turkey. The Greeks and Trojans were at war for ten years.

Zeus – the chief of all the Greek gods. The Greeks believed he was the sender of thunder, lightning and winds.